Original title:
The Magnolia Melody

Copyright © 2025 Creative Arts Management OÜ
All rights reserved.

Author: Theodore Sinclair
ISBN HARDBACK: 978-1-80566-745-2
ISBN PAPERBACK: 978-1-80566-874-9

Lyrical Gardens of Serenity

In gardens lush, a laughter blooms,
A chatty rose with idle fumes.
It tells a tale of sun and glee,
While bumblebees sip tea for free.

A daisy dances on a breeze,
With tiny shoes and wobbly knees.
It twirls and spins, a silly sight,
In shades of pink and pure delight.

Oh, tulips trip on blades of grass,
They giggle soft as passers pass.
Each petal's wink, a joyful tease,
As squirrels laugh and steal some cheese.

In this bright place, where humor reigns,
The flowers speak in funny strains.
With every bloom, a smile shared,
In lyrical gardens, joy is aired.

The Prance of Floral Youth

The sun peeks in, the flowers sway,
With bouncy moves, they start to play.
A wild rose tripped over its thorn,
And laughed so hard it nearly mourned.

Young violets play hopscotch in rows,
Jumping on toes where the wild wind blows.
A clumsy daffodil took flight,
And swirled around, what a silly sight!

Each petals' chatter fills the air,
As bees demand a dance so fair.
They buzz and whirl, no time to sit,
In prance of youth, they just won't quit.

So join the blooms in this delight,
Where every flower sparkles bright.
In floral fun, let laughter bloom,
With nature's joy, we'll all make room.

Blossoms Adrift in Gentle Breezes

Dandelion wishes float high in the air,
While roses film dramas, with secrets to share.
Tulips all giggle, their colors so bright,
As daffodils hum in the warm, sunny light.

A breeze comes to tickle, oh where will it go?
A petal gets tangled in a funny show.
Butterflies dance like they're at a ball,
Then trip on a petal—whoops! Down they fall!

Hymns of the Southern Garden

In the garden of laughter, voices abound,
Where wise old oak trees share wisdom profound.
They crack little jokes that only they get,
While misshapen lettuce ignites a duet.

Sunflowers nod, they just can't stop grinning,
While vines tell tales of their sneaky beginning.
The roses roll their eyes, it's part of the fun,
As petals plot mischief under the sun!

Notes of a Lingering Petal

A single petal plays hopscotch on dew,
With ladybugs laughing like friends, just a few.
The smell of sweet nectar drifts through the air,
As crickets compose tunes without a care.

Each flower a character, all tied in a tale,
They prance with a flair, they dance without fail.
Under the stars, their stories unwind,
In nature's grand show, oh what a find!

Singsong Under the Magnolia

In the shade where petals flirt,
A squirrel sings in an oversized shirt.
Bees in bow ties dance with glee,
While birds debate on who's the key.

Laughter rises on the breeze,
As daisies chat and hug the trees.
A frog in a hat hops around,
Making music, oh so profound.

The Language of Blossoms

Whispers float from blossom to leaves,
'Hey, check my style!' the rose believes.
Tulips chuckle, sharing a tease,
While daisies laugh, 'We're cute with ease!'

Petals gossip, what a delight,
In floral gossip, they take flight.
With each bloom, the punchlines swell,
The garden blooms, a comedy well.

Harmonies of the Heart

In the grove, a chorus plays,
With laughter ringing through the days.
A bumblebee hits all the right notes,
While crickets form their tight-knit coats.

As sunbeams dance on a playful whim,
Flowers sway, with joy they brim.
A butterfly waltzes, laughing loud,
In nature's symphony, they're all so proud.

Celestial Petal Pathways

Strolling through a petal parade,
Where blooms tell tales of charm and jade.
A dandelion sneezes, laughs ensue,
'You flowered so early, what's up with you?'

Stars twinkle, petals join the play,
Creating jokes in their bright ballet.
Underneath the moon's gentle snicker,
Nature's humor grows even thicker.

Whispers of Springtime Petals

Petals drifting in the breeze,
Their dance puts ants at ease.
A squirrel's acorn, now a foe,
Whispers giggles, 'Watch it go!'

Bunnies hopping with great flair,
Trying hard to comb their hair.
Bees buzz loudly, what a sight,
Chasing blooms from morn to night.

Harmonies at Dusk

Crickets croon a silly song,
While frogs sing, 'We all belong!'
The fireflies flicker like a light,
Brought by mischief, pure delight.

A raccoon dons its paper crown,
Declares it king, won't back down.
The moon winks at all the fun,
'Let's stay out 'til day is done!'

Blossom's Embrace

In a garden, blooms converse,
'The sun's back, oh, what's worse!'
Tulips giggle, colors bright,
'Make way for bees, what a sight!'

Dandelions hop on by,
'Let us dance and touch the sky!'
With every toss, they sing aloud,
Springtime's quirks make us so proud.

Sweet Fragrance of Dawn

Morning glories yawn and stretch,
Coffee beans play games, they fetch.
Skunks in boots, a funny scene,
Twirling through the grass so green.

The sun peeks out, lets shadows play,
A giggling lark shouts 'Hip, hooray!'
With every bloom, a chuckle flows,
Nature's punchline, everyone knows!

The Quietude Beneath the Blooms

A squirrel danced beneath the trees,
Chasing dreams with effortless ease.
The blossoms chuckled, bright and loud,
Inviting laughter from the crowd.

A bee buzzed by, lost in the fun,
Trying to join the frolicsome run.
He tumbled down, just like a clown,
Buzzing back up with a silly frown.

The petals giggled, a playful sight,
As crickets sang through the warm night light.
Here beneath, all worries cease,
In this comedy of nature's peace.

Sweet Serenades at Dusk

As dusk approached, frogs took the stage,
Croaking tunes, they laughed with rage.
A firefly stumbled, lit the sky,
Flickering bright like an awkward guy.

The moon peeked out, gave a wink,
While crickets played, not missing a beat.
With each note, the world spun round,
In this symphony of silly sound.

The daisies danced, swayed to the beat,
Stomping petals in shoes of sweet heat.
Nature's odd cast, a comedic thrill,
As stars joined in, just for the chill.

Blossoms Against the Sky

Clouds rolled in, looking so grumpy,
Hiding the sun, feeling all lumpy.
But the blossoms shouted, "Don't lose hope!"
They wore a grin, swinging like a rope.

A bird swooped down in a dive so bold,
Admiring the blooms like treasures of gold.
He fluffed his feathers, struck a pose,
Then tripped on a branch, how the laughter flows!

Buds burst forth, with colors bright,
Creating a canvas in glorious light.
They giggled at clouds, gray and moody,
In their cheeky way, so fruity and foodie.

Petals of Time's Embrace

Time ticked by with a gentle tease,
While petals twirled in the playful breeze.
Each swirl a story, a giggle released,
In nature's humor, joy never ceased.

The sun stretched wide, a toothy grin,
As blooms exchanged tales, cheeky and thin.
A leaf fell down like a dramatic act,
In this comedy show, no moment lacked.

With laughter echoing through the air,
Nature hosted, precious and rare.
In petals of time, a charming embrace,
We find our joy in this whimsical space.

The Sway of Spring's Heart

In a park where pigeons dance,
A squirrel gives a cheeky glance.
Flower hats upon their heads,
Chasing dreams on little threads.

Breezes tease the tulips' pride,
While the ducks just float and glide.
Bumbling bees buzz with delight,
Springtime's stage is quite the sight!

The bunnies hop in silly arcs,
While a frog sings out in larks.
Daffodils and dandelions,
Join the fun in carefree hymns.

With each twist of nature's grin,
Laughter bursts from deep within.
As the sunshine warms the ground,
Joy in every glance is found.

Melodies of Dusty Roads and Blooms

On a walk down gravel ways,
A dog plays tricks, it loves to graze.
Butterflies in fancy dress,
Whirling 'round in spring's caress.

Old man Jenkins sings off-tune,
Arguing with a waving moon.
His cat just yawns with perfect grace,
While robins laugh at his slow pace.

Humble daisies dip and sway,
Competing with the kids at play.
Lemonade stands on each street,
Sipping joy, oh what a treat!

Sunset paints the sky with cheer,
Coloring the world we hold dear.
Each moment filled with joyous glee,
Nature's whimsy sets us free!

Fragrant Memories of Yesterday

In the garden where we'd roam,
Each flower was a little home.
Petunias giggled in the breeze,
As bees tickled the bumblebees.

Grandpa told his funny tales,
Of slippery fish and windy gales.
While grandma danced with spry old shoes,
Each twirl spun laughter, not a snooze.

A picnic spread beneath the sun,
Where sandwiches dared us to have fun.
We spilled juice on the plaid old sheet,
Then chased the ants, our heads a-tweet.

As evening came, with fireflies,
We'd catch dreams beneath the skies.
A fragrant hug from blooms at night,
Summoning joy, pure and bright!

A Tangle of Petals and Stars

Underneath a twinkling sky,
Daisies giggle as stars fly by.
Each petal whispers funny quirks,
While shadows dance with whimsical perks.

A cat debates with a curious frog,
Over who's the better log.
Caterpillars in a line,
Munching leaves with great design.

Fireworks burst in fragrant blooms,
As laughter sweeps away our glooms.
The moon joins in with radiant rays,
Making silly faces, full of praise.

Every twirl in starry night,
Brings a giggle, pure delight.
Amidst the petals soft and bright,
Joy's simple gift—our hearts take flight.

Chants of the Blossoming Woodlands

In the woodlands where we play,
Trees with laughter sway all day.
Squirrels dance in silly ways,
Chanting nonsense, come what may.

Bees in hats buzz by my ear,
Sipping nectar, sipping cheer.
Blossoms giggle, so sincere,
Talking trees lend us an ear.

Frogs in crowns sing odes of spring,
While daisies join in, twirl and swing.
Nature's jesters gathering,
In this wild and joyous fling.

When evening fall, the stars ignite,
The woodland cries, "Oh, what a night!"
With petals falling, pure delight,
In this forest, our hearts take flight.

Symphony of Floral Dreams

In a meadow where dreams bloom,
Flowers plot to chase the gloom.
They wear shades and strut with flair,
Swaying softly through the air.

The daisies play a trumpet tune,
While lilacs whistle to the moon.
Sunflowers waltz, so tall and bright,
Spinning tales of pure delight.

Bugs are drummers keeping time,
With little feet, they dance in rhyme.
Petals twirl in soft ballet,
In this garden, all is play.

A symphony of laugh and cheer,
With blossoms high, there's naught to fear.
Nature's laughs ring far and near,
In the dreams of spring, we're here.

Petals on the Water's Edge

By the pond, petals drift and sway,
Little fish leap in a playful fray.
Frogs do cannonballs, oh what a sight,
As dragonflies zoom with all their might.

Daisies bob, like boats in the stream,
While willows whisper in soft, sweet dreams.
Lily pads laugh, holding on tight,
To the giggles that dance in the light.

Nature's humor is a delight,
Where every splash brings forth a bite.
With petals spinning through the air,
Joyful moments, without a care.

As sunset paints the sky aglow,
Petals twirl in the evening's flow.
In this laughter, we bend and sway,
Together, we'll dance till the end of day.

Leaving Footprints in Blossom

In a field where blossoms grow,
We leave footprints, row by row.
Daisies tickle toes, oh dear!
Laughter echoes, loud and clear.

With every step, we create a tune,
Rabbits hop like they're on the moon.
Flowers giggle, soft and light,
In this garden, hearts take flight.

Butterflies wink with colorful grace,
While we twirl in a silly race.
Petals fly, like confetti bright,
Celebrating this joyful night.

In the breeze, we share a grin,
As the world spins, we all join in.
With footprints left in sweet delight,
We'll dance forever under moonlight.

Garden Serenade

In a garden so bright, the flowers all sway,
The daisies debate who will start the ballet.
While roses roll laughter, so pink and so proud,
They boast of their beauty and sing out loud.

The daisies shout 'Look, we dance best of all!'
But tulips just giggle, then trip and then fall.
In the chorus of blooms, each one claims the song,
Yet, wind plays its tune, and they all get along.

Bees join the tune, buzzing high and so low,
While worms hold a poll in the dirt down below.
The sun starts to chuckle, its rays all around,
And the garden's a stage, with chaos unbound.

The Softness of White Petals

White petals like whispers, they float in the breeze,
As bees on their quest, they buzz with such ease.
A bunny bounds in, to steal a quick snack,
While a squirrel plays drums on an old flower pack.

The petals all shimmy, like they're in a trance,
And the ants start to waltz, oh what a fine dance!
But watch where you step, dear, it's tricky tonight,
As petals become pillows that float in mid-flight.

A robin sees chaos and cackles a tune,
While the clouds start to giggle, they billow and swoon.
The sun grins so wide, like it's been told a joke,
While soft white flowers bloom, and the garden bespoke.

Melodies of the Heartwood

In the heartwood of laughter, the trees tell a tale,
Of acorns that dream and the mighty oak male.
Squirrels in Tuxedos, they play in the bark,
And the woodpecker's rhythm ignites a sweet spark.

The breeze softly teases, the leaves start to wiggle,
While the branches sway close, and the sun starts to giggle.
A raccoon in shades sips his drink on the log,
And the moss joins the dance, looking lush like a frog.

With each twist and turn, the forest hums bright,
The fireflies join in, creating a light.
In this melody made, the trees start to sway,
With nature's own humor leading the way.

Chords of Nature's Lullaby

In the hush of the evening, crickets compose,
A silly little tune with each croak that they chose.
The frogs leap in rhythm, a dance on the stones,
While raccoons in tuxes admire their bones.

The owls start to hoot, a wise old refrain,
As fireflies flicker, a soft glowing chain.
The moon starts to grin, a pale lantern of fun,
While the breeze spins around, a game just begun.

With each chirp and flurry, the night sings a tune,
While shadows do waltzes beneath the pale moon.
In this chord of delight, all creatures unite,
As the world dances on, till the morning's first light.

Symphony of Floral Dreams

Petals dance on breezy tunes,
Waltzing with the light of moons.
The bees hum in a silly race,
While flowers giggle, just in place.

Daisies play their trumpet sounds,
With tulips bouncing all around.
The roses croon, a fragrant show,
As violets blush and join the flow.

Sunflowers stretch to greet the sun,
While daisies peek, just for fun.
The gardener laughs, what a delight,
As colors mingle, oh, what a sight!

So here we sway in floral cheer,
With whimsy's notes ringing clear.
Every bloom has its own dream,
In this symphonic garden theme.

Chants of Nature's Palette

In the garden, laughter grows,
Where wildflowers strike funny poses.
With every breeze, a tickling tease,
Nature's laughter floats with ease.

Chanting with swag, the petals sway,
A comical ballet in full display.
Even the thorns are striking a pose,
As butterflies giggle in their clothes.

Snails wearing hats glide past the blooms,
While grasshoppers rap in little rooms.
The daisies make a lovely wish,
For nature's laughter to be their dish.

Colors clash in a silly jest,
This riot of joy, we love the best.
Splashes of brilliance make us beam,
In nature's palette, we all dream.

The Serene Brush of Floral Strings

With brushes made of leafy greens,
Floral strings play sweet routines.
Tulips strum a playful tune,
While daisies dance beneath the moon.

The sunflowers sway, oh what a sight,
As bees drum beats, buzzing with might.
The violets chuckle, a quiet refrain,
In the garden, laughter does reign.

Petal plucking, a joyful sound,
As nature's orchestra spins around.
Each blossom joins with glee and mirth,
Creating magic upon this earth.

With every note, we skip and leap,
In every flower, a secret to keep.
Harmony blossoms and fills the air,
In the serene brush, we dance without care.

Twilight's Ode to Blossoming Beauty

As twilight wraps the day in glee,
The flowers grin, as if to see.
A silly glow begins to rise,
With sparkles dancing in their eyes.

The peonies boast in shades of pink,
While evening dew makes petals wink.
Sunset colors, a playful tease,
As flowers sway with graceful ease.

Jasmine whispers sweet secrets near,
While laughter lingers in the sphere.
The nightingale sings, a comical tune,
As stars peek out, a radiant boon.

In this twilight, we find delight,
With blooms and chuckles, all feels right.
An ode to beauty, laughter's balm,
In this floral wonder, we find calm.

Haunting Harmonies of the Softest Blooms

In shadows where the garden sleeps,
A chorus of the petals creeps.
They giggle as the moonlight beams,
Sprouting tunes from borrowed dreams.

The daisies dance, the roses jive,
A symphony that's sure to thrive.
The wind's a joker, sly and spry,
Tickling notes while squirrels fly by.

With whiffs of joy, the nectar sings,
As bumblebees play tiny strings.
A serenade from blooming friends,
A laughter that just never ends.

So join the whimsy, take a seat,
In this garden so sweetly neat.
For every petal, every tune,
Will leave you grinning at the moon.

Scented Ballads of the Dusk

At dusk, the flowers hum a song,
While fireflies dance the night along.
The lilacs wink and share a jest,
As crickets chirp, they're feeling blessed.

The peonies sway, with arms out wide,
Singing secrets they just can't hide.
Their fragrances swirl in a playful spree,
Can't help but laugh with glee when you see.

Even the stars join in the fun,
Chatting softly 'til the day is done.
Each petal shows a dash of glee,
As fragrant tales swirl like a spree.

So step outside, don't be a bump,
Join the scented ballad's jump!
Let each bloom tickle your soul,
In fragrant melodies, we find our role.

Elegy for an Unfurling Blossom

An ode to blooms that slowly tease,
With petals popping like a breeze.
They stretch and yawn in morning's light,
In pajamas that glow oh-so-bright.

The buds develop a witty flair,
With whispers traded everywhere.
They giggle at the old oak tree,
"Catch up, old pal! We're wild and free!"

Like comedians in blooming play,
Each bud unfolds in its own way.
With every sigh and every stretch,
A humorous tale, they sketch.

So here's to all those blossoms new,
With laughs in every hue and dew.
An elegy that tickles the heart,
In nature's bloom, we find our part.

Nature's Celestial Orchestra

In the garden's grand amphitheater,
Where blooms are high and banter's sweeter.
The daisies play the flutes tonight,
While sunflowers shine in pure delight.

The bees provide a steady beat,
As butterflies twirl, oh so fleet.
Even the clouds hum a soft tune,
While fireflies blink under the moon.

With petals strumming in the air,
Nature's band is beyond compare.
They're tuning hearts with joyous glee,
A show for all, you and me!

So let the blossoms play their song,
In harmony where we belong.
With laughter echoing through the night,
Nature's music brings pure delight.

Lyrical Blossoms in a Sultry Breeze

In a garden where giggles bloom,
Squirrels tango with brooms.
Laughter rustles through the leaves,
As sunshine pranks and weaves.

Petals dance with silly glee,
While bees buzz a harmony.
Chasing shadows on a whim,
Each flower's a playful hymn.

With a hop and a little twirl,
Daisies join in the swirl.
Echoes of chuckles sway,
As bunnies bounce, frolic, and play.

Underneath the sky so blue,
The blooms share secrets, too.
Their petals spin with delight,
In this comical, sunny light.

Radiance of Petals at Dawn

Morning light tickles the vines,
While sleepy heads laugh at signs.
A wobbly bee takes to flight,
Giggling at his morning plight.

Sunbeams peek through leafy lanes,
Chasing shadows, giving gains.
Each bud opens with a cheer,
As daybreak whispers, 'We're here!'

Lively petals start to sway,
Winking at the break of day.
With a shimmer and a shake,
Joy's the pie they all partake.

Even the wind starts to hum,
As petals jiggle, oh so fun!
A chorus of laughter rings,
From nature's sweet, musical springs.

Blossoms in the Breeze

Winds that tickle bloom-filled trees,
Swaying softly with a tease.
Dancing petals whisper low,
As giggles sprinkle to and fro.

A blossom sneezes, 'Achoo!'
Sending flyaway dreams anew.
Bees roller-skate from bud to bud,
In this cheerful, fragrant flood.

Chasing shadows, chasing light,
What a merry, splendid sight!
Every bloom a jester grand,
With petals waving, hand in hand.

Breezes play their playful notes,
As blooms share their silly anecdotes.
In this garden where we find,
A symphony of joy entwined.

Songs of the Southern Blooms

In the south, where blooms take flight,
Petals serenade the night.
With giggly tunes sung so bright,
Stars waltz in sparkles, pure delight.

Crickets play a tune of yore,
While flowers ask, 'Can we have more?'
A marigold jokes with the moon,
Singing softly, 'Join our tune!'

The honeysuckle's sweet refrain,
Is a cheeky chuckle, never plain.
They tickle swaying willow trees,
In this garden full of glee.

All around, the laughter flows,
As southern air gently blows.
In nature's choir, humor blooms,
With every sweet and sunny tune.

Blossoms Beneath the Stars

Underneath the twinkling night,
A flower danced in pure delight.
It swayed and spun, what a sight!
A tiny bug joined, quite the fright!

The petals blushed, a pink parade,
As bees all buzzed, but could they trade?
The pollen jokes that they all made,
Left everyone in the garden swayed.

Look at them bloom, they're all so spry,
They call out to the moon with a sigh.
"Hey up there, could you give it a try?
With a wink and a laugh, we'll fly high!"

With laughter echoing through the night,
The flowers kept dancing until first light.
A bust of petals, what a silly plight,
The garden's a party, oh what a sight!

A Symphony of Blooming Dreams

A whistle here, a hum there too,
The flowers form a ragtag crew.
They gathered 'round for a song to brew,
And boy, did they know just what to do!

The daisies played their trumpets bright,
While violets danced in sheer delight.
"More marigold, this feels just right!"
A tulip twirled, what a joyful sight!

With laughter trailing in the breeze,
They warmed the night with cheeky tease.
"I dare you to climb the tallest trees!"
Said one bold petal with comical ease.

As melodies rang through the air,
Each flower claimed a moment rare.
They laughed till dawn, without a care,
A blooming circus, beyond compare!

Echoes in the Shade

In the shade where shadows play,
Tiny frogs croak, "Hey! Come this way!"
A bunny hops with nothing to say,
While daisies get tangled in a game of sway.

"Stop that tickling!" the lilacs shout,
As grasses weave, there's no doubt.
A squirrel joins, trying to scout,
To join this floral game, what a clout!

In whispers, leaves conspire and snicker,
As roots swap tales that come out quicker.
"Why not wear leaves? They're quite the sticker!"
The laughter bursts—nature's own flicker.

Echoes of fun in dappled light,
Where blooms and critters share delight.
Each small adventure takes flight,
Creating giggles throughout the night!

Gentle Hues of Spring

Gentle hues awaken and tease,
As flowers throw their petals with ease.
The bees are buzzing, "Oh, what a breeze!"
While lazy cats lounge under the trees.

"Why, oh why, do you wear that hat?"
Said a cheeky bloom to a sunny cat.
"I'll wear my best if you promise that,
We'll throw a party that's nice and fat!"

Daffodils swayed in a happy trance,
While tulips blushed, "Invite us to dance!"
Mirth in petals, what a great chance,
As everyone gathered, it's quite the romance!

With laughter floating from flower to flower,
The garden sparkled, hour by hour.
In this bright and lively bower,
Spring's funny charm turned hearts to power!

Silhouettes in Soft Light

Beneath the trees, we dance and sway,
A squirrel mocks our every play.
The moonlight giggles, shining bright,
As shadows join our silly fright.

The branches shake, a gentle tease,
As breezes tickle with such ease.
We wander paths of laughter, free,
Chasing shadows, just you and me.

A chipmunk claps, a crowd of one,
He thinks our antics are such fun.
In twilight's glow, we burst in cheer,
Oh, what a night, the stars appear!

The world a stage, we take our bow,
With laughter loud, we're here, and how!
In these soft lights, we find delight,
As nature giggles, pure and bright.

Voices in the Arbor

Whispers swirl among the leaves,
While critters plot their pranks and schemes.
A rabbit grins, a crow surveys,
The joy of jest in leafy bays.

With every rustle, secrets fly,
A chorus sings, the branches sigh.
We join the fun in playful chase,
Our voices mingle in this space.

The owls roll eyes, they're quite the pros,
As we re-enact our favorite shows.
Each giggle bounces, fills the air,
In this tall realm, we shed all care.

Laughter echoes, bright and clear,
While moonlit pranks bring us near.
In the arbor's embrace, we play,
As silly sounds take night away.

A Whisper Through the Branches

A gentle breeze brings chatter low,
With every whisper, secrets flow.
We gather round in leafy shades,
As laughter spills, the charm invades.

The crickets join, a quirky band,
With unsteady beats, we take the stand.
A wily fox raises a brow,
At our wild antics, oh, wow!

With branches swaying to and fro,
We dance along, a breezy show.
The night erupts with joyous sounds,
As we tumble 'mongst the golden grounds.

Each rustle laughs, each leaf a smile,
In nature's arms, we stay awhile.
So come, dear friend, let's share the night,
With whispers sweet and pure delight.

Murmurs of Magnolia Evenings

In evening's glow, we craft our tales,
As night winds weave through fragrant trails.
With every giggle, joy takes flight,
In murmurings that feel just right.

Fireflies blink, a winking troupe,
While shadows skip in merry loop.
We crown ourselves with flowered crowns,
As wild laughter roams the towns.

A nightingale hums, a comic sound,
While blossoms dance all around.
With every twirl, our hearts embrace,
In this spectacle, we set the pace.

So here we stand, with spirits bright,
Embracing whims in the moonlight.
In whispers soft, we find our play,
As magnolias giggle the night away.

Sweet Surrender of Spring Light

In springtime's dance, the blooms do jest,
They tickle the air, they bloom their best.
The sun whispers secrets, a cheerful tease,
As petals play tag with the buzzing bees.

With each fluttering leaf, we giggle and grin,
The grass gets tickled, it starts to spin.
Dandelions wear crowns, jesting so bold,
While tulips gossip tales of new buds to hold.

The daffodils laugh, in yellow delight,
As daisies twirl under warm golden light.
Snapdragons grin, with mouths open wide,
In this springtime circus, there's nowhere to hide.

So let's dance through the gardens, with laughter in tow,
For spring's a jester, putting on quite a show.

Flourish of Beauty in Every Note

The lilacs hum softly, a sweet serenade,
While roses compose in a floral parade.
Each blossom a note in a whimsical tune,
As violets sway gently, beneath the bright moon.

Petunias do jiggle, they burst into song,
With each petal bouncing, they can't go wrong.
The tulips are twirling, like dancers in line,
While sunflowers bob, keeping perfect time.

There's music in colors and laughter in scent,
As bees buzz along, in floral content.
A symphony woven in petals and leaves,
In gardens alive, where each blossom believes.

So let us embrace this melodic display,
And dance in the bloom, till the end of the day.

Wildflower Whispers and Magnolia Sighs

In fields of wildflowers, whispers abound,
They share silly secrets from under the ground.
Magnolias chuckle, with petals so wide,
While daisies tease bees, with a wink and a glide.

The clover comes laughing, a jolly green friend,
In gatherings cheerful, where giggles don't end.
Poppies parade in their bright scarlet best,
While pansies just giggle, forgetting the rest.

The breeze takes a trip, with stole and a hat,
It stirs up the weeds, in a mischievous spat.
And all of us join in the silly old game,
With laughter and blooms, never the same.

So let the wildflowers take us for a spin,
With giggles and sighs, let the season begin.

Poets of the Blossom's Heart

In gardens of poets, where verses take flight,
Each petal's a word, in the soft morning light.
The orchids compose, with a delicate grace,
While the willows write sonnets, in their leafy embrace.

The sun dares the daisies to rhyme with the bees,
As lilacs narrate tall tales in the breeze.
Hydrangeas gather, their colors a show,
While the jolly old daisies put on a big glow.

Laughter erupts with each stanza they spin,
As phlox tosses petals, inviting a grin.
Every bloom tells a story so vibrant and true,
In this whimsical world of poetic debut.

So gather, dear friends, in this blossoming art,
For we're all poets in the blossom's heart.

The Garden's Silent Song

In the garden where daisies dance,
A bee sings silly in a glance.
The roses giggle, oh so bright,
While the sun winks, shining light.

A snail in shades takes a long stroll,
Claiming the title of 'Garden Goal.'
While flowers gossip, oh so sly,
Trading secrets with the sky.

Caterpillars sporting tiny hats,
Wobble like tipsy acrobats.
The sunflowers laugh as they sway,
Hoping to brighten up your day.

So join the fun, don't delay,
In this garden where laughter plays.
Nature's humor in full bloom,
Lighting up the happiest room.

Flowering Truths

In a patch of celestine blue,
A marigold tells jokes anew.
The lilies chuckle, petals wide,
While crickets take a buggy ride.

Petunias plotting pranks at dusk,
Inventing ways to be a musk.
The ferns just roll, with leaves outspread,
Whispering tales of laughter fed.

Dandelions blow their fluffy dreams,
Creating wishes with silvery gleams.
The tulips tease the passing bees,
Chasing them round the swaying trees.

So join the party, give a cheer,
In this garden, fun is near.
With every bloom, a secret glee,
Nature's truths set laughter free.

Garden of Echoing Smiles

Beneath a arch of leafy vine,
A lily laughs, saying, "Oh, I'm fine!"
With petals soft and fragrance sweet,
It spreads the joy where all can meet.

A gopher dives for treasures lost,
His snickering spirit shows the cost.
Nature's folly is here to stay,
With critters dancing, come what may.

Morning glories stretch and beam,
Competing for the brightest dream.
The daisies jive in cheerful style,
Creating rhythms, mile by mile.

So stroll through paths of smiles so wide,
With flowers blooming side by side.
In this garden, laughter rings,
Echoes of joy that nature brings.

Serendipity in Bloom

In a field where giggles sprout,
Butterflies float, swirling about.
A clover gives a playful wink,
While bumblebees flirt and think.

The poppies dance atop the hill,
Swaying with a carefree thrill.
A dandelion takes a puff,
And giggles as it calls the bluff.

In hidden corners, laughter brews,
As petals share their vivid views.
A ladybug steals the show,
With polka dots in charming row.

Celebrate this joyful space,
Every corner holds a grace.
With serendipity unfurled,
In blooming fun, joy is twirled.

Echoes of the Southern Woods

In the woods, the squirrels play,
Chasing shadows, night and day.
They steal my snacks without a care,
Nature's rascals, unaware!

A bird sings high, off-key refrain,
Its notes are wild, a silly strain.
The frogs join in, a croaky tune,
A chorus fit for a cartoon!

Trees sway gently, dancing slow,
While bugs perform a comical show.
They trip and tumble, what a sight,
Nature's antics, pure delight!

So next you stroll where the wild things leap,
Just laugh and giggle, don't you weep.
For in these woods, with joy you'll find,
A symphony that's sweetly blind!

Petal Dances in Twilight

In twilight hours, the flowers prance,
Their petals twirl in a silly dance.
With a breeze that's soft as feathered play,
They laugh and giggle, come what may.

The bees buzz round with clumsy grace,
In this garden, it's a funny race!
They bump and bounce from bloom to bloom,
Creating chaos, brightening gloom.

A rabbit hops by with a flashy wig,
It wiggles and jiggles, oh so big!
With every leap, it sprays out cheer,
A goofy fella, always near!

As stars peek out, the night grows bold,
These floral jesters remain uncontrolled.
They celebrate with a whiff and a spin,
In a vibrant world of laughter within!

Lullabies Beneath the Magnolia

Beneath the tree, a snore resounds,
A possum dreams of wild, sweet hounds.
While crickets play a lullaby tune,
The fireflies dance around the moon.

The raccoons hold a midnight feast,
With stolen fruits, they're quite the beast!
They sip on juice, with laughter loud,
As sleepy critters form a crowd.

The bumblebees, they sway and sway,
Too full of nectar, they drift away.
With little hiccups and a buzz,
Night serenades, just because!

As the world sighs in slumber deep,
These woodland jesters just can't sleep.
With giggles echoing far and wide,
Nature's funny hearts, side by side!

Serene Soprano of Nature

In nature's choir, the voices blend,
With squeaks and squawks, there's no pretend.
A serenade of silly cheer,
Bringing smiles to all who hear.

A turkey gobbles, thinking it's cool,
While frogs croak jokes, breaking the rule.
They sing of love, and silly tales,
Chasing their dreams with flailing tails.

As owls hoot in a regal pose,
They watch the antics of squirrel shows.
With every jump and jolly twist,
They join the fun, impossible to resist!

So listen close, beneath the boughs,
For nature's laughter, oh, it allows.
A whimsical tune in the moonlit night,
The orchestra of joy, pure delight!

A Tapestry of Floral Lullabies

In gardens where giggles bloom,
Petals dance in bright costume.
Bees buzz like they're in a band,
Riding sweet notes across the land.

With each sway, the branches tease,
Tickling toes in the spring breeze.
Flowers gossip, sharing tales,
Of bumbling bugs and fairy trails.

Nectar drips like honeydew,
As butterflies put on a show too.
A hummingbird hits the high note,
Dancing like it's on a boat.

In this symphony of cheer,
Nature's humor draws us near.
We laugh at every quirky scene,
In this floral stage, so serene.

Songs of the Swaying Branches

Swaying branches tell their jokes,
As squirrels sip tea with the folks.
They giggle at the budding bloom,
Turning every heart to zoom.

The breeze carries silly rhymes,
Singing softly through the pines.
Each twig taps like a playful hand,
Directing laughs across the land.

Petals flutter in delight,
Winking at the morning light.
Even shadows join the fun,
Playing hide-and-seek with the sun.

Amidst this lively, cheerful spree,
Nature's tunes are pure and free.
With every leaf a little grin,
The joy of life is found within.

The Scent of Gentle Reminiscence

Whispers float on floral air,
Gentle scents without a care.
Each bloom holds a secret laugh,
In gardens where the memories draft.

Swinging by with fragrant cheer,
Witty words that all can hear.
Violets share their sweetest woes,
While daisies poke their little toes.

As we roam through this sweet place,
Laughter paints a floral face.
Every petal seems to tease,
Echoing fun beneath the trees.

In this space of soft good cheer,
Even the thorns can crack a sneer.
Joy is sweeter than we think,
As nature winks and starts to blink.

Harmonies of Blooming Radiance

Radiant blooms in playful rows,
Conduct tiny acts of prose.
Blossoms burst with vibrant glee,
As if nature made a decree.

Each flower hums a different tune,
Tickling the air like a cartoon.
Petals prance on sunlit stage,
Displaying nature's joyous page.

The sun dips low, a actor shy,
While clouds drift by like popcorn high.
With laughter rolling down the lane,
Every leaf knows how to entertain.

In the night's enveloping cloak,
Stars join in as the breezes poke.
Even frogs croak in harmony,
Adding to the fun we see.

Songs of the Silver Leaves

In the garden where the breezes tease,
A squirrel sings, with startling ease,
He struts around, a real show-off,
While birds join in, to scoff and scoff.

Petals fall like little hats,
On sleepy dogs and lazy cats.
They wonder what all the fuss is,
While chasing dreams, just like the whizz.

Bumblebees borrow tunes from the trees,
They buzz and hum with the utmost glee.
Frogs leap in with a croaky laugh,
Joining the fun, they're a perfect half.

So celebrate the laughter here,
Where everything is sweet and clear.
Raise a glass to this crazy spree,
Floral music for you and me.

Floral Reverie Underneath the Stars

Under a sky that winks and glows,
The flowers dance, as everybody knows.
Petals swirling, a show of style,
With funny hats that make you smile.

A raccoon insists he leads the way,
With twirls and leaps that steal the day.
Laughter echoes through the night,
As everyone joins this pure delight.

Crickets chirp in a quirky tune,
While fireflies blink like stars in June.
The moon chuckles at their flair,
As flower friends take to the air.

So sway along, beneath the skies,
Where every giggle composes ties.
Join the party, oh what a blast,
With blossoms dancing, having a blast!

Dance of the Fragrant Bloom

In the garden where giggles grow,
The flowers shout, 'Hey, look at me go!'
With petals waving like hands in cheer,
They beckon all to come and steer.

Tulips twist in a vibrant spin,
Daisies jump, let the fun begin!
A bumblebee dons a little crown,
While butterflies flit in a fancy gown.

The sun peeks in, with a cheeky grin,
As blooms perform their lovely spin.
Against soft winds, they laugh and sway,
Turning this garden into a play.

So dance along with flowers bright,
Join their joy, it feels so right.
With every twirl, they make it clear,
That laughter blooms, and life is dear.

Lullaby of the Garden's Heart

In the hush of night, the flowers hum,
Whispering tales of what's to come.
A dandelion yawns, it's time to rest,
While sleepy blooms wear their nightie best.

Butterflies snuggle in leafy nooks,
Reading stories from classic books.
The vines chuckle at the silly dreams,
As starlight spills in golden beams.

A wise old tree tells a joke so grand,
That even the moon gives a knowing hand.
In this lullaby of petals deep,
Nature's laughter will never sleep.

So close your eyes, let the garden sing,
As funny whispers of breezes bring.
Rest easy, dear, as the flowers play,
In the night's embrace, till break of day.

Moonlit Gardens

In gardens bright with shades of green,
The critters dance, a silly scene.
A raccoon wears a jaunty hat,
While squirrels debate who looks more fat.

The moon looks down, quite round and grand,
Laughing softly at this strange band.
A flower sneezes, bees take flight,
While fireflies twinkle, oh what a sight!

Beneath the trees, the shadows play,
All creatures join in the nighttime ballet.
A frog hops on, with a croak so bold,
Claiming the spotlight, or so he's told!

With giggles shared in the moonlight bright,
The garden thrives in the night's delight.
So join the fun, bring a chair or two,
In this whimsical world, there's room for you!

Notes of a Summer's Eve

As sun bids adieu, the laughter flows,
A racquetball rolls where no one goes.
The neighbors gather, drinks in hand,
Sharing tales that are not quite so planned.

The kids play tag, oh what a sight,
While Grandma naps, dreaming of flight.
A dog snores loud, it's quite absurd,
Each snort a chord, in this summer bird.

Lemonade spills in vibrant hues,
While music plays, confusing the blues.
An impromptu dance on the grass so green,
Turns into chaos, but it's quite the scene!

As evening falls with stars aglow,
The laughter lingers, the good times grow.
Under the sky, no care in sight,
Just a summer's eve, full of delight!

Beneath the Blooming Canopy

Under blooms bright, the chatter swells,
Of flowers that gossip, oh the tales they tell!
A daisy insists she's the fairest of all,
While the roses just roll, thinking she's small.

Bumbling bees with their buzzing sound,
Self-proclaimed kings of the garden ground.
They flit and they float, in search of the best,
While butterflies giggle, thinking they jest.

A fern in the corner, all frilly and green,
Watches the antics, a most curious scene.
With roots firmly planted, it holds in a grin,
While critters and flowers delight in their spin.

Under this canopy, mischief and cheer,
The humor of nature feels perfectly clear.
So come take a seat, join the whimsical fun,
Beneath the bright blooms, you'll see how it's done!

Rhythms of Quiet Moments

In cozy corners where the sunlight glows,
A cat with a yawn, in soft repose.
The clock ticks slow, a rhythmic delight,
While shadows play peek-a-boo with the light.

Tea cups clink, an old lady's jest,
As she recounts tales, each one a quest.
Her teapot whistles a tune so sweet,
While cookies dance in a merry little beat.

Outside the window, a butterfly flits,
Making the moments feel like soft skits.
A breeze whispers secrets, soft as a sigh,
As all of life's rhythms pass gently by.

With a chuckle or two shared over pies,
Quiet moments become the grandest of highs.
So slow down, take heed, let laughter chime,
In these small stillnesses, you'll find the rhyme!

Sweet Notes from the Tree Canopy

In a breezy dance, they twirl and sway,
The petals giggle, come out to play.
Squirrels in tuxedos, prance so spry,
While birds in bowties sing to the sky.

Honeybees buzzing, oh what a buzz,
Mistaken a tree for an all-you-can-rub.
Each blossom is fancy, clad in white crème,
They laugh at the wind, a floral-themed dream.

They knock on the boughs with a gentle thud,
A little bird says, "This tree's full of bud!"
With laughter and joy, the canopy sings,
Nature's own party of whimsical things.

So sit by the trunk, and join in the rhyme,
As laughter rings out, in a tree so sublime.
Perhaps you'll find friends; they're waiting for you,
In the sweet silly symphony held in the blue.

Crown of Blossoms

A crown of petals atop the tall tree,
Wobbling and giggling, carefree as can be.
Bees in a frenzy, they buzz and quirk,
While ants join the dance with a skip and a smirk.

The trunks wear their grins, carved smiles so bright,
As birds chirp jokes in the soft morning light.
Flowers start spinning, a whimsical trend,
While leaves sway along, nodding, my friend.

Oh what a ruckus, in this leafy affair,
With honey and laughter, there's fun in the air.
A squirrel steals the show, in grandiose style,
With acorns for props, oh, he's worth your while!

So tip your hat, to the crown that is bold,
A show of delight, it never gets old.
Join in the merriment, don't miss the spree,
In this hilarious realm, where blossoms roam free.

Chorus of Light

The sunlight bursts through, a musical cue,
The branches laugh out, in a radiant hue.
With petals that twinkle, like stars on a spree,
The blossoms all chime, "Come dance with me!"

Bumblebee choirs, in harmony buzz,
"Please hand us some pollen!"—it's quite the fuss.
Grasshoppers leap with a flip and a flair,
While ladybugs waltz, without a care.

With every soft rustle, a funny old tune,
Leaves sway so sweetly, beneath the round moon.
The laughter of nature, an echo so bright,
In the chorus of light, let's dance through the night!

So gather your friends, in this jamboree,
Where the flowers are jesters, and life's filled with glee.
Join in the laughter, let your spirit take flight,
In the harmony blooming, of a world clothed in light.

Melodies from the Magnolia's Embrace

In a hug full of blooms, such sweetness we find,
The fragrance a giggle, tickles the mind.
With petals unfurling, in playful delight,
The tree shakes its branches, "Let's party tonight!"

A chipmunk in shades, struts to the beat,
While bunnies breakdance, with rapid little feet.
The whispering leaves join in, swaying along,
As laughter erupts like a jubilant song.

Drifting through whispers, a breeze full of cheer,
The flowers all chuckle; "More cake, my dear?"
Nature's own feast, and the drinks made from dew,
As blossoms all cheer, "We're so glad to see you!"

Let's twirl in the air, with joy wrapped around,
In this whimsical world, where laughter is found.
With each petal's embrace, your heart will delight,
In the melodies woven, from day into night.

Petal Whirlwinds of Delight

Whirlwinds of petals, a carnival scene,
Nature's confetti, pink, white, and green.
With every soft rustle, the flowers exclaim,
"Catch us if you can!" in this whimsical game.

A ladybug slips, on a sail made of leaf,
Cursing the wind for this moment of grief.
While crickets compete in a footrace so fast,
With giggles that echo, they want this to last.

A butterfly twirls, sporting clothes that are bright,
With antics so funny, it's pure delight.
As petals keep swirling, dance partners unite,
In the joyful chaos, everything feels right.

So let's join the fun, in this loop-de-loop day,
With nature's bright wonders, come laugh and play!
In the petal whirlwinds, let your spirit take flight,
In a world full of laughter, where hearts shine so bright.

www.ingramcontent.com/pod-product-compliance
Lightning Source LLC
Chambersburg PA
CBHW071822160426
43209CB00003B/173